What's the difference?
Amphibians

Stephen Savage

RSVP

RAINTREE
STECK-VAUGHN
PUBLISHERS
A Steck-Vaughn Company

Austin, Texas

www.steck-vaughn.com

What's the difference?

Amphibians   Insects
Birds   Mammals
Fish   Reptiles

Cover: A red-eyed tree frog and (below) a northern red salamander

Title Page: A common frog swimming and (inset) a fire salamander

Contents page: A leopard frog leaping out of a pond

Published by Raintree Steck-Vaughn Publishers, an imprint of Steck-Vaughn Company

Printed in Italy. Bound in the United States.
1 2 3 4 5 6 7 8 9 0 04 03 02 01 00

Library of Congress Cataloging-in-Publication Data
Savage, Stephen.
Amphibians / Stephen Savage.
    p.   cm.—(What's the difference?)
    Includes bibliographical references and index.
    Summary: Describes the physical characteristics common to amphibians and highlights differences among various species, discussing habitats, methods of getting around, feeding habits, and how amphibians reproduce.
    ISBN 0-7398-1359-5 (hard)
    0-7398-2038-9 (soft)
    1. Amphibians—Juvenile literature.
    [1. Amphibians.]
    I. Title.
    QL644.2.S28 2000
    597.8—dc21   99-044321

Contents

What a Difference!

Amphibians can live on land and in water. A few kinds of amphibians live entirely in the water, and some live only on land.

Not all amphibians look the same. Newts and salamanders have four short legs and a tail. Frogs and toads have two short front legs, two long back legs, and no tail.

▼ The African goliath frog is very large. It can grow up to 14 in. (35 cm) long.

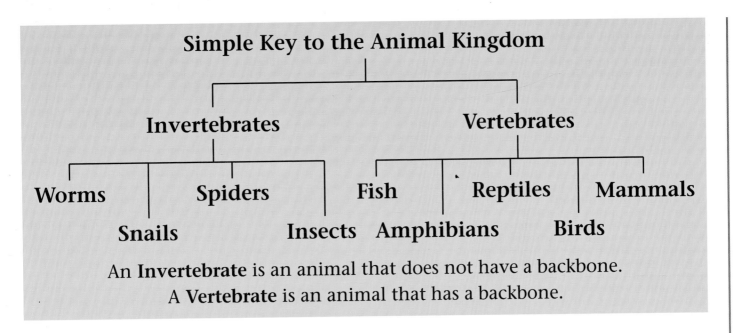

Simple Key to the Animal Kingdom

- **Invertebrates**
  - Worms
  - Snails
  - Spiders
  - Insects
- **Vertebrates**
  - Fish
  - Amphibians
  - Reptiles
  - Birds
  - Mammals

An **Invertebrate** is an animal that does not have a backbone.
A **Vertebrate** is an animal that has a backbone.

Amphibian characteristics

- Many amphibians have eyes on top of their heads.
- Most have four legs.
- They have to keep their skin damp.
- Most adult amphibians breathe with lungs.
- Young amphibians (tadpoles) breathe with gills.

The bright colors of this tiny poison arrow frog warn other animals that it is poisonous.

Where Amphibians Live

Amphibians must have water to survive. They live mostly near lakes, streams, and ponds. Some live in rain forests. There water collects in large leaves, and the forest floor is damp and mossy.

▼ The red-eyed tree frog lives in the trees of tropical rain forests. Like all tree frogs, it has toe pads, which help it cling to large shiny leaves.

Amphibian habitats

- Amphibians that live in cold climates hibernate in winter.
- Spade-foot toads live in burrows in the desert.
- In many countries, building development has reduced natural areas of wetland. There, more common frogs are in garden ponds than in the wild.

▲ The water-holding frog leaves its desert burrow only during the short rainy season.

Some frogs and toads can survive in deserts. They spend most of the year living in underground burrows.

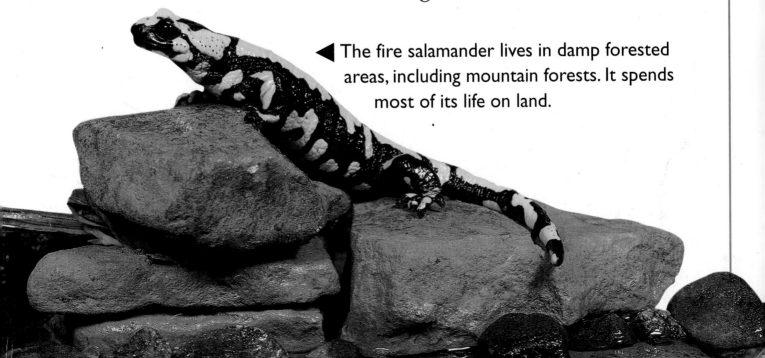

◄ The fire salamander lives in damp forested areas, including mountain forests. It spends most of its life on land.

Catching a meal

Amphibians feed on different kinds of prey. Some eat tiny animals. Some larger amphibians can eat bigger prey, such as small mammals, lizards, and fish.

◀ This frog is flicking out its long, sticky tongue to catch an insect grub. It catches worms, spiders, and slugs in the same way.

◀ This Australian cane toad is swallowing a small mammal.

Most frogs and toads use their sticky tongues to catch prey on land. When they are tadpoles, living in water, they can eat only plants.

▼ This American bullfrog eats mice, snakes, and small turtles as well as fish and insects. Like most frogs it can draw its eyes back into its head to help it swallow a large meal.

Newts and salamanders feed on land and in water. On land they eat worms and insects. They can wipe the dirt off a worm with their feet before swallowing it.

In water, newts and salamanders eat tiny water animals, tadpoles, and insects.

▲ The horned toad looks like a dead leaf on the forest floor. It pounces on unsuspecting prey, which includes insects, lizards, and mice.

Avoiding danger

- Most amphibians are camouflaged to blend in with their surroundings.
- Many hide during the day and are active only at night.
- Some amphibians have skin that is poisonous to predators.
- Some can puff their bodies up to look larger.

This common newt ▶ is hunting for insects among damp leaves in a woodland area.

▲ Salamanders use their tiny teeth to catch worms, which they swallow whole.

Hot and Cold

Amphibians are cold-blooded. This means that their body temperature changes with the temperature of the air or water around them.

▲ The common toad hunts at night. Then the air is cool, and its prey comes out to feed.

◀ On a hot, sunny
day, the common frog
returns to the cool
water of a pond.

Many amphibians remain
hidden during the day to avoid
the sun's heat. A few survive in
deserts by living underground
and near waterholes.

▼ The desert-living spade-foot
toad can absorb water through its
skin. It comes out of
its burrow in the
rainy season.

In countries where winters are very cold, amphibians can hide away and sleep to survive the cold. This is called hibernation.

▲ This common frog is hibernating in a hole. It will sleep all through the winter.

Hot and cold facts

- In cold areas, the tadpoles (young) of American bullfrogs may take up to two years to become adults.

- In warm winters common frogs may lay their eggs as early as Christmas Day.

- A hibernating frog breathes only through its skin.

A hibernating common frog can live in temperatures as low as 21° F (–6° C), which is well below freezing.

When the weather is cold, tadpoles ▶ may take longer to develop into adults.

▼ Frogs living near water sometimes like to warm themselves in the sun.

Getting Around

Amphibians move around in various ways. Frogs and toads either hop, leap, or crawl, while their tadpoles wriggle through the water.

Many amphibians have webbed feet that help them swim. A few types of amphibians never leave the water.

▼ Clawed toads spend all their lives in water. They swim using their strong back legs and webbed feet.

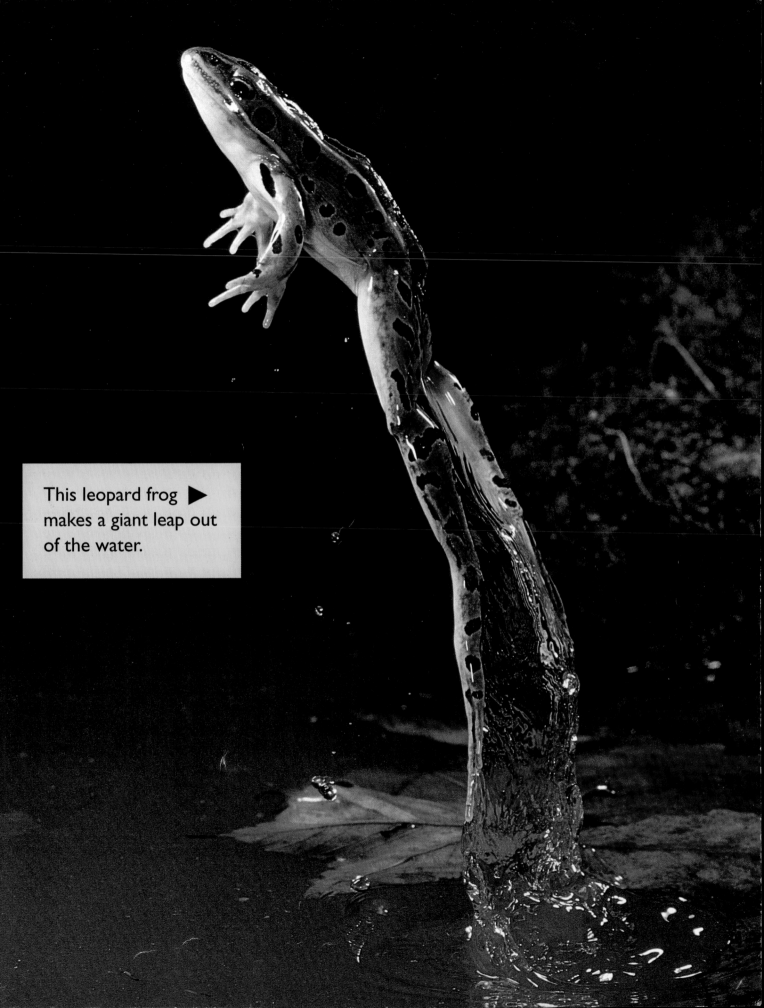

This leopard frog ▶ makes a giant leap out of the water.

Newts and salamanders use their four legs to crawl on land. They can also walk along the bottom of a pond.

▼ The Alpine salamander uses its strong tail to help it swim.

▼ The Costa Rican flying frog can glide up to 100 ft. (45 m) from one tree to another, using its webbed feet as parachutes.

Two kinds of tree-living frogs can actually glide through the air. They can travel great distances to escape danger.

Moving about

🐸 A newt swims using its tail and a wriggling movement of its body.

🐸 Frogs can leap away from danger.

🐸 The common toad migrates a long distance each year to reach the pond where it will breed.

🐸 American bullfrogs can leap up in the air to catch bats.

◀ This red salamander walks on its four short legs, looking for prey.

Amphibian Young

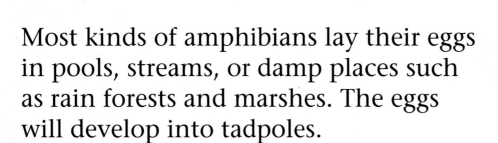

Most kinds of amphibians lay their eggs in pools, streams, or damp places such as rain forests and marshes. The eggs will develop into tadpoles.

▼ These frogs are mating, and the female is laying eggs, protected by jelly. The eggs will soon become tadpoles.

Frogs and toads use croaking sounds to attract a mate. Newts and salamanders choose a mate by performing a courtship dance.

▲ This African painted reed frog is calling to attract a mate, using its balloon-like vocal sac.

◀ Newts return to the water to breed. These two are performing a courtship dance.

Frogs and toads lay all their eggs in one place. Some newts lay their eggs one at a time and carefully hide each one.

Some amphibians lay their eggs in very unusual places. A few give birth to live young.

▼ These gray tree frogs have made a communal foam nest to protect their eggs. The tadpoles will drop from the nest into a pool below.

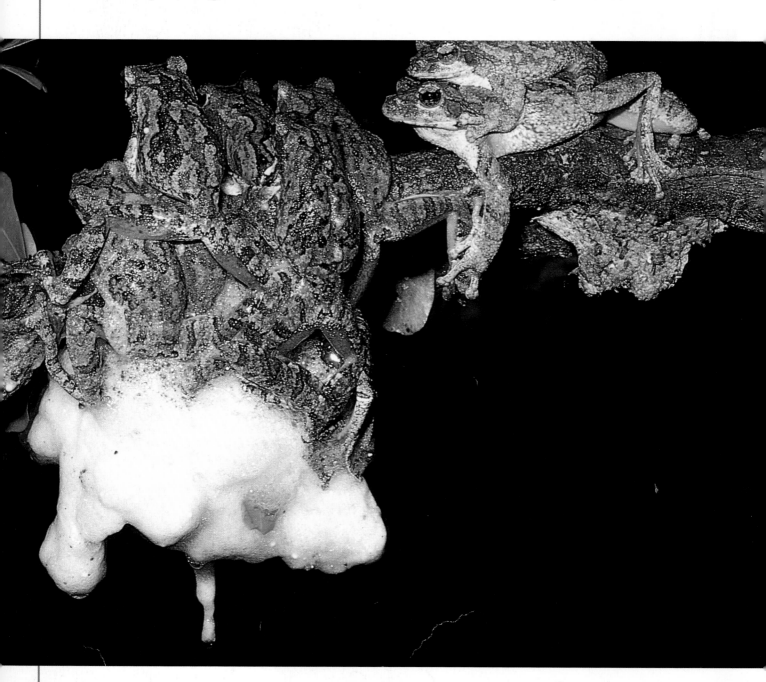

Facts about young amphibians

The eggs of the Alpine salamander hatch inside the female's body and are born as tiny adults.

The eggs of the female midwife toad are carried by the male for a month before they hatch.

▲ The female Surinam toad takes great care of her eggs. She carries them on her back.

Life cycle of a frog

1. Eggs

6. Adult frog

5. Grows front legs and loses tail.

2. Tadpole hatches out of egg. Breathes with gills.

3. Loses gills and grows lungs.

4. Grows back legs.

Pet Amphibians

Frogs, toads, and newts often live in garden ponds. This is usually the best place to see them and watch their tadpoles developing into adults.

▼ This common toad is sheltering in a flower pot. Many toads and frogs live in gardens, especially if there is water nearby.

Caring for pet amphibians

🐸 Amphibians are not easy to look after. If you keep them in an aquarium, make sure it has a lid.

🐸 Provide a land area of rocks, soil, and branches as well as water.

🐸 Adult amphibians need to eat food that is live.

🐸 The aquarium should be lit with "daylight" bulbs.

Most adult amphibians are difficult to look after. However, they are sometimes kept in an aquarium. This must have a land area so that the animals can leave the water.

The larval salamander lives in water, ▶ breathing through its gills. After about two months, it will be fully developed, with lungs to breathe on land.

▼ This fire-bellied toad is showing its red belly as a warning that it is poisonous.

Unusual Amphibians

Many amphibians look quite strange to us. Some of them live in unusual places.

◄ The caecilian is different from other amphibians. It has no legs and lives in an underground burrow, where it eats worms and insects.

Unusual facts

- The Cuban tree frog is the smallest amphibian. It is about half an inch (12 mm) long.

- The tadpole of the paradoxical frog is four times larger than its parents, growing up to 10 in. (25 cm) long.

- If a young great crested newt loses a leg to a predator, it can grow a new leg.

- Just .035 oz. (1 g) of poison from a poison-arrow frog could kill 100,000 people.

- Although the axolotl never develops from the tadpole stage, it produces young.

▲ The Japanese giant salamander grows to 5 ft. (1.5 m) in length. This salamander never leaves the water.

The axolotl is a type of salamander. It has feathery gills like a tadpole, and it never develops out of this form. It lives all its life in water.

◄ The axolotl is like a giant larval newt that never grows up.

Scale of Amphibians

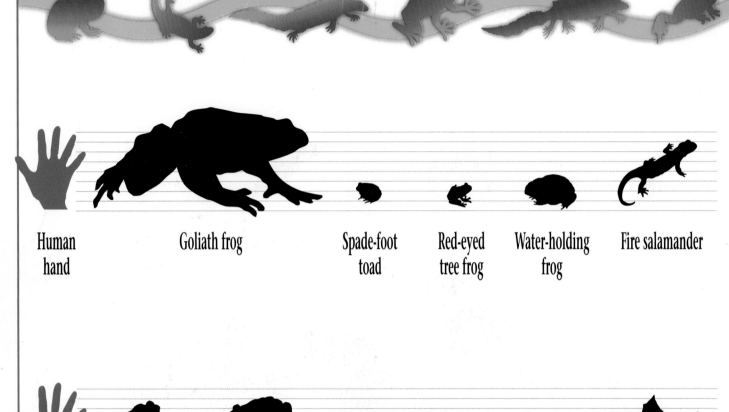

Human hand   Goliath frog   Spade-foot toad   Red-eyed tree frog   Water-holding frog   Fire salamander

Human hand   Australian cane toad   American bullfrog   Horned toad   Common toad   Common frog   Clawed toad

Human hand   Leopard frog   Red salamander   Costa Rican flying frog   Gray tree frog   Surinam toad

Midwife toad

Fire-bellied toad

Caecilian

Paradoxical frog and tadpole

Great crested newt

Human hand

Axolotl

Japanese giant salamander

Human hand

Poison-arrow frog

Common newt

Alpine salamander

African painted reed frog

Cuban tree frog

Human fingertip

Glossary

Algae A type of plant growing in water.

Aquarium A large tank for keeping water animals and plants.

Burrows Holes dug in the ground by animals for shelter.

Camouflage Protection from attack by appearing to be part of the surroundings.

Communal Shared by others.

Courtship dance A dance performed to attract a mate.

Gills Organs for breathing.

Hibernate To spend the winter in an inactive state resembling sleep.

Larval Describing young amphibians between the egg and adult stage. At this stage they are also commonly called tadpoles.

Migrates Moves from one place to another, to find food, to mate, or to escape from the cold.

Predators Animals that hunt other animals for food.

Prey Animals that are hunted and killed for food.

Salamander A kind of amphibian that lives more on land than in water.

Tadpoles The larvae (grubs) of amphibians after they have left the eggs. They live in water, breathing through gills, while they develop into adult amphibians.

Vocal sac A pouch that some frogs can fill with air to help them make a variety of sounds.

Books to Read

Theodorou, Rod. *Amphibians* (Animal Babies). Portsmouth, NH: Heinemann Library, 1999.

Miller-Schroeder, Pat. *Scales, Slime, and Salamanders: Reptiles and Amphibians* (Science at Work). Austin, TX: Raintree Steck-Vaughn, 2000.

Greenaway, Theresa. *Tadpoles* (Minipets). Austin, TX: Raintree Steck-Vaughn, 2000.

Nathan, Emma. *What Do You Call a Baby Turtle?* (What Do You Call a Baby...). Woodbridge, CT: Blackbirch Press, 1999.

Kalman, Bobbie and Jacquilene Langille. *What Is an Amphibian?* (Science of Living Things). New York: Crabtree, 1999.

Index

Page numbers in **bold** refer to photographs.

Picture Acknowledgments:

Bruce Coleman /Stephen Doyle 7(t), /Hans Reinhard 7(b) and title page (inset), /Kim Taylor 8(t), /Jane Burton 13(t) and title page, /John Cancalosi 13(b), /Jane Burton 15(t), /Hans Reinhard 16, /Robert Maier 18, /Jeff Foott Prod. cover (inset) and 19(t), M.P.L. Fogden 19(b), 22, /Jane Burton 25(t), 27(b); Frank Lane Picture Agency / S. Maslowski 9, /Derek Middleton 20; NHPA /Daniel Heuclin 4, /Kevin Schafer 5, /Daniel Heuclin 11, /Stephen Dalton 12, /G.I. Bernard 14, /Daniel Heuclin 21(b), 23, /B.A. Janes 24, /Jany Sauvanet 26, /Daniel Heuclin 27(t); Oxford Scientific Films 15(b), /John Netherton 6, /Kathie Atkinson 8(b), /Michael Fogden 10(t), /David Boag 10(b), /Stephen Dalton 17 and contents page, /Michael Fogden 21(t), 25(b); Tony Stone Worldwide /Tim Davis cover (main picture). Artwork on page 23 by John Yates and on pages 28-9 by Mark Whitchurch.